THE LORD OF THE RINGS

THE RETURN OF THE KING

VISUAL COMPANION

THE LORD OF THE RINGS

™

THE RETURN OF THE KING

VISUAL COMPANION

JUDE FISHER

HarperCollins*Publishers*

THE GREAT TASK

A Fellowship of Nine Companions set out from the Elven haven of Rivendell, charged with a grim and perilous task: to carry the One Ring – an artefact of great power – across Middle-earth and destroy it in the fires of Mount Doom before it can fall into the hands of the Dark Lord, Sauron. With the last and greatest of the Rings of Power in his grasp, his dominion will spread across all the world and his shadow will fall over all the Free Peoples of Middle-earth. Already, cruel armies have encroached into erstwhile peaceful territories, harrowing the lands and murdering all in their path.

On their journey, two of the company perished: Boromir, son of the Steward of Gondor, and Gandalf the Grey, an Istari wizard. Two of the company, the hobbits Merry and Pippin, were carried off by Uruk-hai warriors and borne away towards the stronghold of the wizard Saruman, at Isengard. The rest of the companions split into two groups: the hobbits Frodo Baggins and Samwise Gamgee continuing the quest to destroy the Ring alone, save for the lurking presence of the ambivalent creature, Gollum; while Aragorn, heir to the kingdoms of Men, Legolas, son of King Thranduil of the Mirkwood Elves and the Dwarf Gimli, son of Glóin, set off to rescue the abducted hobbits.

5

While traversing the rocky peaks of the Emyn Muil, Frodo and Sam capture Gollum and make a pact with him: he will lead them into Mordor, through the secret ways he discovered when escaping from Barad-dûr; and in return they will not harm him. But Gollum still craves the Ring he once possessed, for the Ring corrupts all who bear it: even Frodo is not immune to its seductive power. Gollum is prey to a terrible internal struggle: to serve Frodo faithfully in memory of that part of him which once was Sméagol; or to relinquish himself to evil.

In the fair lands of Ithilien, which lie between the great River Anduin and the Mountains of Shadow, Frodo and Sam are set upon by Rangers captained by Faramir, brother to Boromir and son to Denethor of Gondor. Like his brother, he sees the Ring as a valuable tool: a weapon which may give Men the advantage they so desperately seek against the Enemy; he takes the hobbits prisoner, meaning to deliver them into the hands of his father and thus win his much sought-for approval. But under attack in the ruined city of Osgiliath, and moved by Frodo's grim plight as Ringbearer, he relents and allows the hobbits to continue on their quest. They are close to Mordor now, with only the Mountains of Shadow to cross. Gollum claims to know a secret way through to the other side. It seems unlikely he can be trusted, but they have no other choice than to take him at his word and follow him.

Aragorn, Legolas and Gimli pursue the Isengard Orcs on foot across the Plains of Rohan, only to encounter a pile of burning corpses of Uruk-hai and the band of horsemen which dispatched them, a troop led by Éomer, nephew to the King of Rohan. Of Merry and Pippin there is no sign. But under the eaves of the forest of Fangorn, Aragorn discovers tracks which suggest the pair may have survived the rout, and so they enter the ancient woodland. Once inside this eerie place, it is not Merry and Pippin they find, but a figure in shining white: Gandalf the Grey may be no more, but having finally destroyed the Balrog which dragged him from the Bridge of Khazad-dûm, he has returned transformed. Now, he is Gandalf the White, and he is mightier than he ever was before.

Merry and Pippin had indeed escaped the evil grasp of their captors and plunged into the safety of the forest, only to encounter what seems an even greater danger: a vast, treelike being which towers over them and grabs them up into its woody hands. This is Treebeard, the Ent, a herder of the beleaguered trees of Fangorn and one of the most ancient beings to walk the face of Middle-earth. The Ents have little trust of strangers left now in this part of the world, and Treebeard has never before encountered such a thing as a hobbit.

Meanwhile, Saruman's war-efforts on behalf of the Dark Lord continue apace. Having whipped the dispossessed Dunlendings and Wild Men into a frenzy of vengeance, he has sent them out, along with great bands of Uruk-hai warriors, to scour the kingdom of Rohan. Once Rohan falls, the last kingdom of Men – Gondor – lies at the mercy of the Shadow. But Saruman does not rely solely on the depredations of his motley army to defeat the kingdom of the horse-lords: for he has set a spy within its very heart. In the Golden Hall of Meduseld, in the Rohan capital of Edoras, Gríma Wormtongue sits at King Théoden's right hand, pouring words of poison into his ear, even to the extent of banishing the true-hearted Éomer. Aged beyond his natural years, his wits addled by sorcery, Théoden is no longer the heroic leader his people require in their hour of need, and now that Éomer has been removed, Rohan lies defenceless.

Knowing Merry and Pippin to be with the Ents, Gandalf, Aragorn, Legolas and Gimli make for the Courts of Edoras, where Gandalf releases King Théoden from Saruman's sorcerous influence and Gríma Wormtongue is cast out, released to crawl back to his master's abode. As the spell is removed, the years and senility fall away from the King, until at last he is himself again, restored to his wits, his strength and the knowledge of the magnitude of his task: to save his people from

rout and ruin. Their only hope now is to retreat to the safety of Helm's Deep, the great fortification created by the ancient hero, Helm Hammerhand. While Gandalf searches for Éomer and the Rohirrim who remain faithful to him, the Rohan refugees must be led by the Lord Aragorn across moor and mountain, plain and pasture, where they will be beset by war-parties of Orcs and wargs. But a far greater danger will soon be at hand: a vast army of Uruk-hai is on the march from Isengard: the defenders of Helm's Deep will find themselves hopelessly outnumbered, unless other allies can be found.

The time of the Elves in Middle-earth is at an end. Their numbers have dwindled, their powers are fading. Most have already left the shores of this world for a life of eternal bliss in the Undying Lands across the Sea. Their last alliance with Men ended in disaster – the

death of many of their kind in vain. The weakness and greed of Isildur betrayed the short victory over Sauron, for instead of destroying the One Ring when he had the chance, Isildur decided to keep it for himself. That decision has led to destruction and despair: it is not surprising that the Elves are reluctant to come to the aid of Men once more. Moreover, when an Elf loses his life, he loses eternal life: to do so for the sake of Men would be a great sacrifice indeed.

It is also a sacrifice which Arwen, daughter of Elrond, will have to make if she is to stay in Middle-earth and marry the Lord Aragorn. Such a decision requires the utmost courage and conviction, and an unshakeable faith in the future of the world.

Yet, on Lord Elrond's instruction, Haldir of Lórien brings a force of Elven archers to the aid of the defenders of Helm's Deep. Once more, Men and Elves stand side by side to face a shared enemy and what seems almost certain death. It is a grand gesture, and for a while it holds the inexorable tide at bay. But Haldir falls in battle, and the Uruk-hai keep advancing. All seems lost, despite great heroism from the defenders. At the dawn of the fifth day, however, Gandalf the White and the Rohirrim crest the mountain peak above Helm's Deep and charge down the scree to crash headlong into the flanks of the Uruk army. At last the tide is turned and the Orcish

army broken. Men live to fight another day in Middle-earth. Helm's Deep has been a great victory, but the War of the Ring has only just begun, and there are many more battles to be fought, on many fronts.

Elsewhere, the forces of Light are at work, as the Ents of Fangorn are finally roused to ire against Saruman, who has destroyed so many of their kin. They march upon Isengard and there take their revenge, breaking the dam to flood the mines and forges around Orthanc Tower, taking apart the White Wizard's evil work piece by piece with the slow, inexorable power of root and branch.

But as the Ringbearer and his faithful companion, Sam Gamgee, make their way ever deeper into the Land of Shadow, the heavier and more burdensome to Frodo the Ring becomes, dragging him down, exhausting him with the weight of its evil and its intent to return to its Master, whose presence becomes more dreadful and more tangible with every step they take. And as they approach their goal, the hatred and mistrust between Gollum and Samwise Gamgee grows ever greater. In the end, it may not be Orcs or Nazgûl, or even Sauron himself, which threaten the success of the quest, but the struggle that is going on within the soul of the creature once called Sméagol…

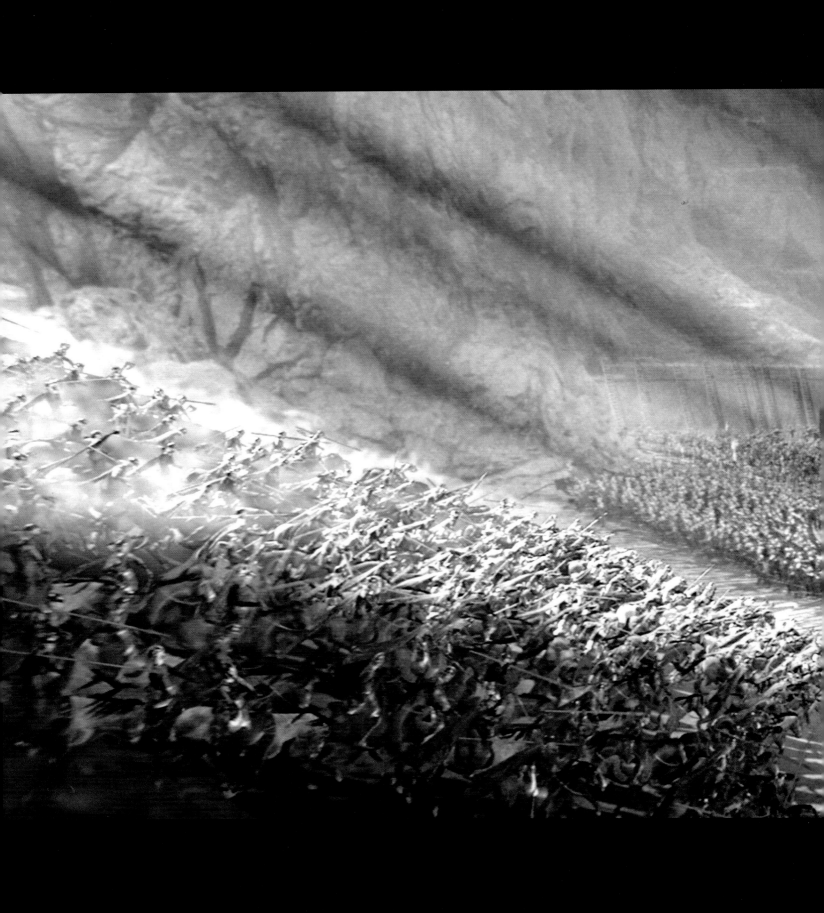

THE KINGDOM OF GONDOR

South and east of the Kingdom of Rohan, and closest of all to Mordor, lies Gondor, the great kingdom of Men which was founded by Elendil in the Second Age of Middle-earth. In elder days, it counted amongst its chief cities Osgiliath, Minas Tirith and Minas Ithil and the ports of Dol Amroth and Pelargir; but Minas Ithil was lost to the Nazgûl and is now known as Minas Morgul, and Osgiliath has become little more than an outpost of war. Through millennia, war and plague have decreased Gondor's power and its population, and after the failing of Elendil's line, the kingdom has had no king. Gondor is no longer the mighty and glorious realm it once was.

MINAS TIRITH

"Mordor: this city has dwelt ever in sight of that shadow"

Where the White Mountains come to an end in the great peak of Mount Mindolluin, there lies Minas Tirith, the City of Kings. It is a vast and elegant city, built in seven levels of white stone which have been carved into the hill so that it looks less a creation of men's hands, but a settlement hewn out of the very bones of the earth by giants. Each level is ringed by a wall and battlement and a gate set into each wall at different points, so that the paved road which climbs towards the seventh level zigzags its way to the summit. The topmost circle rises more than seven hundred feet above the Great Gate which is set into the first circle, and the view downward is sheer and vertiginous.

At the summit lies the Citadel, which contains the High Court, the Place of the Fountain and the White Tower of Ecthelion, where the white banner of the Stewards flutters a thousand feet above the plain.

Minas Tirith is a mighty fortification: apparently impregnable, for there is no access into the city save by the Great Gate of Gondor at its base, which is well guarded indeed. At its back Mount Mindolluin rises sheer and its lower skirts are hedged with ramparts right up to the unscalable precipice. Its walls are high and massively thick, unconquerable by steel or fire, and its battlements afford cover to archers: it is the greatest stronghold in all of Middle-earth.

"It is before the walls of Minas Tirith that the doom of our time will be decided!"

THE GUARDS OF
THE CITADEL

Tall ships and tall kings

Three times three

What brought they from the foundered land

Over the flowing sea?

Seven stars and seven stones

And one white tree.

14

The Guards of the Citadel are robed in black, and their glittering silver helmets are tall and high-crowned and are made from mithril, that most beautiful and priceless of metals, mined by the Dwarves. Light and hard, it could be beaten like copper and polished like glass, and its sheen would never tarnish. These marvellous helmets have long cheek-guards which fit close to the face, and above the cheek-guards are set the white wings of sea-birds, in memory of the days of yore, when Elendil and the ancestors of men sailed to Middle-earth from Númenor, the westernmost of all mortal lands. The guards' black surcoats are embroidered in white with a blossoming tree beneath a silver crown and seven stars. This is the livery of all the heirs of Elendil and is now worn in all of Middle-earth only by the Citadel Guards of Minas Tirith. The seven stars represent the stars figured on the sails of the ships, bearing the seven seeing-stones, which brought Elendil and his people from Númenor.

THE WHITE TREE

Isildur, son of Elendil, who saw his father die on the field of battle against Sauron, and who cut from the Dark Lord's hand the One Ring, planted a sapling from the seeds brought from his homeland in Númenor in memory of his brother, Anárion. But in later days, the tree withered and died, so that now before the pretty fountain in the white-paved courtyard it is a sorrowful sight indeed; black and broken and barren, a fitting symbol indeed for the kingless realm of Gondor in its sad decline.

THE STEWARDS OF THE KINGS

When the line of the Kings failed, the Stewards became the official rulers in Gondor and passed the title down from father to son for hundreds of years. Although appointed to hold the kingdom in charge until the rightful king shall come and claim the throne, such a great span of time has now elapsed that there is no longer any belief that a king shall return, and the Stewards have become increasingly arrogant and king in all but name.

Nevertheless, the Stewards never sit on the ancient throne of Gondor itself, but on a plain, black stone chair at its foot in the chilly, high-vaulted great hall of Minas Tirith. They wear no crown or robes of office and carry only a simple white stave as a token of their rule, rather than any kind of sceptre; and their banner – which flies from the top of the Tower of Ecthelion – is of plain white, where the royal banner, like the insignia of the Citadel Guards, has a sable ground and bears the image of a white tree capped by seven stars.

"The rule of Gondor is mine, and no other's!"

The current Steward of Gondor is Denethor, son of Ecthelion, father to Boromir and Faramir. He is an old man now and time and grief have etched deep lines on his proud face. Denethor has learned too much of the lore of the world – from the great library of Minas Tirith, and from gazing into the surviving seeing-stone in the White Tower. As a result, he knows more than any save Gandalf of the horrors they face in the War for Middle-earth, but the peril of possessing such knowledge is that it can give way to despair, and thence to madness.

"Boromir was loyal to me and no wizard's pupil!"

The discovery of the death of his eldest son, Boromir, has already diverted his noble mind from a sane course, and in his grief he has turned against his younger son, Faramir, so that it seems there is nothing the young Captain of Gondor can do to win his father's

16

younger son out to retake the fallen city of Osgiliath against overwhelming odds is surely a fool's mission and one which must surely result in Faramir's death.

THE TOMBS OF THE STEWARDS

"The houses of the dead are no places for the living"

On the Hallows, the silent shoulder of rock between the mountain and the citadel there is a great domed chamber in which no breath stirs. Inside, draped with shadow, rows of tables carved from marble line this grim hall, and on each sarcophagus lies a sleeping form, hands folded on its chest. These are the Tombs of the Stewards, where the remains of the dead lie interred in crumbling grandeur like grey ghosts. It is a place of great veneration: for the people of Gondor now seem to accord more reverence to the dead than to the living.

approval. That Faramir allowed Frodo Baggins to carry the One Ring into Mordor, rather than bringing it back to Gondor to be used as a weapon in the war against Sauron, is something his father cannot forgive. Yet to send his

OSGILIATH

"No army of Sauron has ever crossed the Anduin, not while men of Gondor
have held the passage of the river"

On either bank of the Anduin stand the ruins of a once-mighty city, the two sides of which are linked by an ancient stone bridge which spans the Great River. Known by the Gondorian people as Osgiliath, it was called 'the Citadel of the Stars' by the Elves, and in the elder days was the capital city of the kingdom of Gondor.

Over the passing of the centuries, after the depredations of war and plague had taken their toll on the population, the folk of Gondor gradually moved away from Osgiliath, abandoning it to the forces of age and time until little of its magnificence and grace remained.

18

Towers were cast down, statues tumbled; weeds sprang up through the cobbled stones of its streets. Now, as a new and terrifying conflict shadows the Third Age of Men, it has fallen into total disrepair and been transformed into a place of utter desolation; and its western side has become a frontier of war.

Eastern Osgiliath has fallen into the hands of the forces of Mordor: Orcs and Wargs and other fell creatures roam the ruins. But the western part of the city is patrolled by the Ithilien Rangers, Men of Gondor under the captaincy of Faramir, son of Denethor of Minas Tirith.

If the Enemy can overcome this last-ditch defence, Gondor lies at the mercy of Sauron's army, and the great city of Minas Tirith will be the only hope left to Men before the Shadow falls over all the Free Peoples of Middle-earth.

19

THE RETURN OF THE KING

"Gondor has no King..."

Although the Stewards and people of Gondor have lost faith in the possibility of the return of a king to rule their realm, a distant scion of the royal house still exists, one of the shadowy ancient people of the North, the Dúnedain. As a sign of his heritage he wears the Ring of Barahir, an heirloom of the house of Beren One-hand. He was known to the hobbits first as Strider; then in Rivendell was his true identity revealed: Aragorn, son of Arathorn, heir of Isildur of Gondor.

22

Many challenges has Aragorn had to meet and face on the long road to his return; and the sternest are yet to come. As the shadows deepen and need is greatest, the second token of his kingship shall be brought to him.

THE SWORD REFORGED

From the shards of Isildur's ancient sword, Narsil, which cut from the Dark Lord's hand the One Ring in the great battle which ended the Second Age, and which has until now lain in Rivendell, has come the Sword Reforged – Andúril, Flame of the West! Made by the Elven-smiths, it bears seven stars, a crescent sun and a rayed moon and its blade is carved with runes.

"Sauron will not have forgotten the sword of Elendil… The blade that broke shall return to Minas Tirith"

It is now time for Aragorn to reveal himself to the Dark Lord, through the palantír of Orthanc, the seeing-stone which Gandalf bears, for to know that the heir of Isildur lives and walks the earth will be a sore blow to Sauron's heart and may further distract his Great Eye away from the Ringbearer on his perilous trek toward the Mountain of Fire.

THE PALANTÍR

But instead Sauron offers Aragorn a terrible vision: of his beloved, pale and lifeless, reft of her Elven immortality. The Evenstar, the glittering jewel which Arwen gave to Aragorn as a token of their love, shatters. Far away across Middle-earth, the effect of this sorcery is felt: the power of the Evenstar is broken. But to embrace a life on Middle-earth and live as a mortal with her love was the choice which Arwen had already made. Even Sauron's malice cannot destroy their love.

23

THE PATHS OF THE DEAD

"Every path you have trod through wilderness, through war, has led to this road.

This is your test, Aragorn…"

In the Second Age of Middle-earth the Men of the Mountains swore an oath to the last King of Gondor at the Black Stone of Erech that they would come to his aid to fight against the Dark Lord; but when his need was desperate, they fled away into the Haunted Mountain, the Dwimorberg. And so Isildur cursed them: that they should never rest in peace until they had fulfilled their oath. Now Aragorn, Isildur's heir, must call them to their oath, to aid the Free Peoples of Middle-earth in their dire struggle against the Shadow.

"The dead are following... I see shapes of men and of horses and pale banners like shreds of clouds, and spears like winter thickets on a misty night"

The road to the Dimholt is ominously silent: in that haunted place nothing stirs, neither wind nor bird. At the root of the mountain gapes a dark door like the mouth of night. Signs and figures are carved above its wide arch, and fear flows from it like a grey vapour. No one living who has stepped through this door has returned alive; but Aragorn, Gimli and Legolas enter with grim resolve. Ghastly, bony hands clutch at them out of the chill darkness; fog swirls; voices wail. All around them are the Dead: their King and row upon row of his spectral warriors. As they gather for attack, Aragorn draws the Sword Reforged and claims their allegiance anew, promising in exchange for their duty that he will release them from their living death. They listen; and they follow...

SAURON

The Dark Lord's history has long, deep roots. He entered the world as a Maia (as did the Istari wizards – Saruman and Gandalf – in a later age) under the direction of the Valar, those purest of spirits, and his task was to tend to the world's good. But Sauron fell under the influence of Morgoth, a Vala who had betrayed his fellows and embraced evil and the pursuit of dominion. Thus was Sauron seduced into his allegiance. As Morgoth's servant, he learned much of evil and power, and following the Great Battle which ended the First Age, in which Morgoth was at last cast down by the Valar, he fled to Middle-earth and there began his reign of terror.

He established himself in the dread realm of Mordor, east of the River Anduin and separated from Gondor, the nearest kingdom of Man, by the Mountains of Shadow. There he began the construction of a mighty tower from which he might look out over his own province and the world beyond, which he sought to ensnare. In the long centuries which followed, Sauron set himself to corrupting the races of Elves and Men and devising a plan by which he might bring dominion of all the Free Peoples of Middle-earth under his control. First, he laboured with the Elven-smiths to create the Rings of Power: nine for the Kings of Men, seven for the Dwarves and three for the Elves. But some time afterwards he treacherously forged for himself a ruling ring in the heart of Orodruin, the Mountain of Fire; and sorcerously imbued it with a great deal of his magical power. But the Elves evaded his trap, and the Rings proved to have little effect on the Dwarves; the Men, however, proved weak and fell quickly under his influence.

Using the power of the One Ring, Sauron completed his great tower of Barad-dûr and drew his forces about him. When his treachery became clear, war was inevitable. The Elves

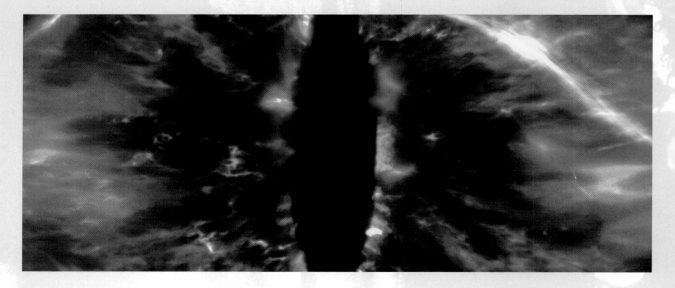

took arms against him and cast him down; but he was not completely defeated until the great Battle of Dagorlad, which ended the Second Age of Middle-earth, when Isildur, son of the fallen King Elendil, cut the One Ring from Sauron's hand. Reduced to a fiery spirit form, and a great, ever-seeking Lidless Eye, Sauron retreated and set himself to the task of rebuilding his forces: a matter which proved far more difficult without the One Ring which, until a hobbit called Bilbo Baggins came by it following an encounter with the creature Gollum, remained lost even to his searching Eye.

But in the Third Age, as his servants travelled far and wide across Middle-earth, word came to him that the Ring was in a small rural backwater known as the Shire. There he sent his Black Riders, the nine Nazgûl on swift black steeds, and the quarry was flushed out into the open. Many times have his servants come close to retrieving the One Ring; and now it is making its own way towards him, through the borders of his Shadow Land: he senses its presence, and the Ring answers. It travels with two hobbits and their guide, the slinking spy, Gollum, who once escaped from the dungeons of the Dark Tower and must therefore know well the return route. What hope can they possibly have in the face of the odds which await

them? Tens of thousands of Orcs, Uruk-hai, Trolls, Haradrim, Easterlings, Mûmakil, fell beasts and the Nine Riders has he gathered about him for an army: to enter Mordor with the Dark Lord's most precious possession is surely to walk into his very arms, and the destruction of the free world.

BARAD-DÛR

"Towers and battlements, tall as hills…"

Once he had forged the One Ring, Sauron used the power with which he had invested it to create the greatest fortress in Middle-earth, and he named it Barad-dûr: the Dark Tower. Here, at the south end of the Mountains of Ash, in the midst of the volcanic Gorgoroth Plain in the dread land of Mordor, he might dwell and further his treacherous plans for dominion. Fell runes and evil sigils denoting the sorcery with which it was made cover its towering black walls. It is a place of untold horror.

From the torture chambers in its dungeons, in which racks and wheels are manned by cruel Orcs, its fiery factories of war, its eyeless prisons and mighty courts, to the vast iron crown at its apex, Barad-dûr climbs thousands of feet into grim skies, as massive and forbidding as any mountain peak. And between the spiked iron pinnacles at the top of the tower, the Great Eye shimmers, constantly awake and aware, constantly seeking the Ring and the one who bears it.

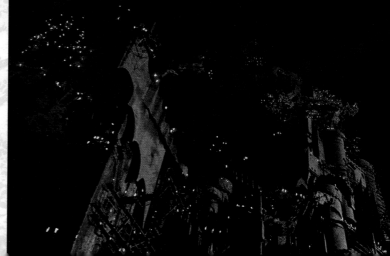

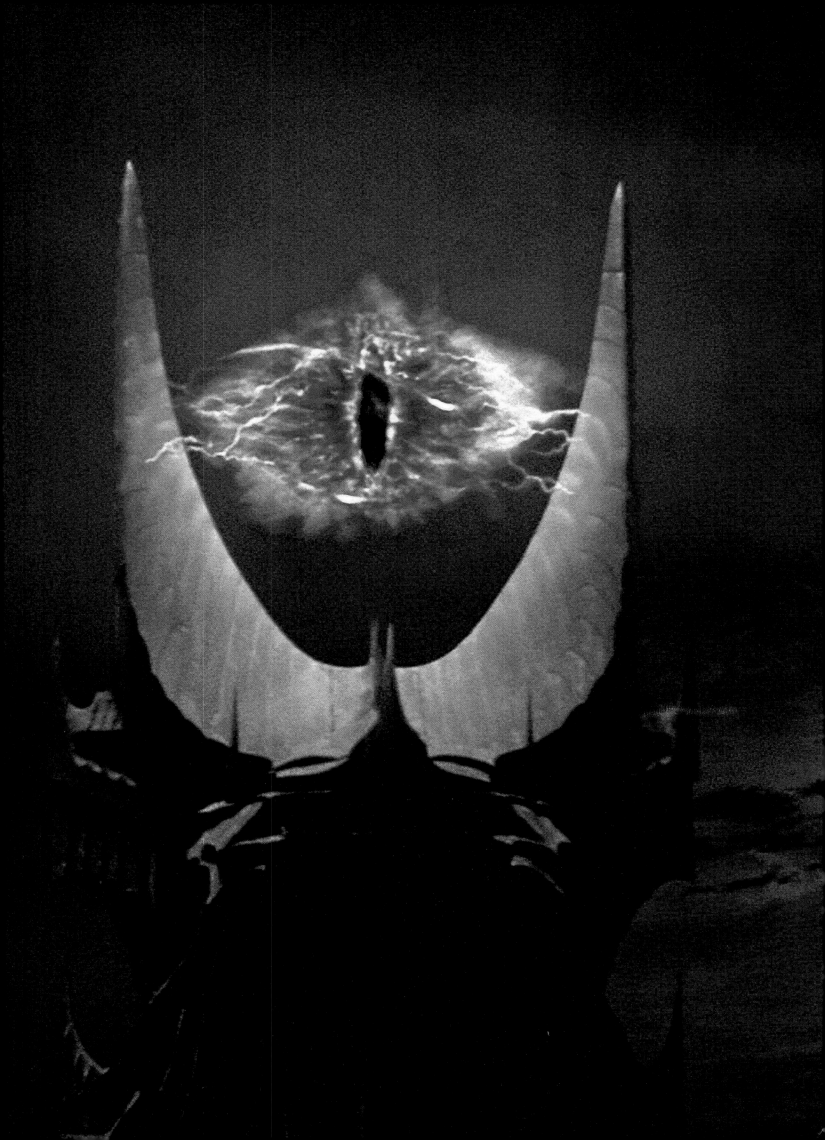

NAZGÛL

"They once were Kings of Men…"

In the Second Age, Sauron ensnared nine Kings, proud rulers of the Men of Middle-earth, by gifting each of them with a Ring of Power and promising them long life and endless power. And thus, being Men and weak of will, they fell prey to his sorcery and were corrupted so that their mortal essence fell away and they became wraiths, destined to live in the world as undead creatures, bound always to his servitude.

They appear dressed all in flowing black robes and rusted mail, and carry long swords; where their faces should be is only darkness; but their true selves, which can be seen only by one wearing the Ring, is spectral and fearsome indeed. As wreathing, tormented beings all of tattered grey and white they are, their expressions distorted by the greed and grief of their condition; their crowns a mockery of the honour and rule they have lost.

The Nine are known also as Ringwraiths and as Black Riders when, mounted on vast black steeds, they searched far and wide through the Shire for the one called Baggins, who was rumoured to have in his possession the Ruling Ring. As Frodo, bequeathed the Ring by his Uncle Bilbo, and his companions made their way from Bree to Rivendell, they encountered the Ringwraiths at Weathertop, where Frodo was stabbed with a sorcerous Morgul-blade, a terrible wound which would trouble him until the end of his days.

Their home is Minas Morgul, the Tower of Black Sorcery, where their shrieking cries pierce the

32

night and strike chill fear into the hearts of any who hear them. Most terrifying of the Dark Lord's servants, no man can kill them; although, perhaps because of some vestige of their once-mortal selves, they are afraid of fire.

FELL BEASTS

Having lost their steeds in the floods of Bruinen below Rivendell, the Nine Riders have come by more terrible mounts by far. As Sam, Frodo and Gollum cross the Dead Marshes, a huge winged shape swoops overhead, gliding soundlessly across the wide mere. This new horror is a fell beast out of Mordor – a huge, black, naked thing, its vast, leathery wings stretched between the wide span of its bony fingers like the wings of some monstrous bat.

It is a creature of an older world, one of those which bred in cold mountain eyries and were taken and nurtured on nameless foods by the Dark Lord until they grew larger than any other flying thing.

Mounted on such a creature, the Nazgûl can travel at great speed and oversee every part of Sauron's realm. Nothing can hide from them...

THE WITCH-KING OF ANGMAR

"The most fell of all his captains..."

The Lord of the Ringwraiths, and the mightiest servant of the Dark Lord, is the Witch-king of Angmar. Greater than the other Nazgûl, he dresses all in sable, save for a silver helm which flickers with perilous light.

Of his origins, little is known except that he was once a king and a sorcerer, but he was ensnared by Sauron when he received the greatest of the Nine Rings. After Sauron's fall in the Battle of Dagorlad at the end of the Second Age of Middle-earth, he fled into the shadows and thence to the lands between the Ettenmoors and the Northern Waste, where he created for himself the realm of Angmar, and there became known as the Witch-king of Angmar.

In later times he and the rest of the Nine Riders took control of Minas Ithil and renamed it Minas Morgul, Tower of Black Sorcery, and there he remained until called upon by his lord, who in the Third Age had regained some of his former power. Sent out to regain the One Ring from the hobbit, 'Baggins', he struck down Frodo at Weathertop, dealing him a terrible wound with his sorcerous blade.

As the commander of Sauron's dark forces, it is the Witch-king who, clad in black armour and helm and armed with sword and flail, leads the great host out of the gates of Minas Morgul at his master's bidding, over the bridge and away west to war in Gondor, to lay siege to the fair city of Minas Tirith, where, against all likelihood and prophecy, he will meet his doom.

"His own folk quail at him, and they would slay themselves at his bidding..."

34

HARADRIM

"Very cruel wicked Men… Almost as bad as Orcs…"

From the South comes a fierce race of Men, inhabitants of a realm of Harad. For millennia they have warred with Gondor, even when defeated remaining a threat on the kingdom's borders. Tall and dark and cruel, they are fearsome warriors, especially when armed with their wickedly sharp spears.

MÛMAKIL

"Grey as a mouse,
Big as a house..."

Their greatest advantage in war is the use of mûmakil (in singular, mûmak) – known also by the hobbits as Oliphaunts – which bear great war-towers packed with Haradrim archers into the midst of battle, trampling and crushing their enemies, men and horses alike, under their massive feet, their spiked tusks swaying perilously, impaling those in their way.

In the Battle of the Pelennor Fields, in the fields outside Minas Tirith, these fierce warriors and their fighting mûmakil will be deadly foes to face for the soldiery of Gondor and the Riders of Rohan.

ENGINES OF WAR

The forces which the Dark Lord has amassed and which will now bear down upon Gondor are vast and terrifying: endless columns of Orcs and Uruk-hai, trolls and unnamed monsters; an army of Haradrim and their massive, fighting mûmakil fitted out with great war-towers manned with archers; and above them all the Nine Riders swoop and dive, mounted on their vile fell beasts. It is an army to drive a chill into the heart of the surviving Men of Gondor, now gathered inside the mighty fortress city of Minas Tirith.

The city is said to be impregnable; but so it was believed of the ancient stronghold of Helm's Deep, which nevertheless was breached by Saruman's army of Uruk-hai with their ballistas and ladders and their great battering ram, which broke down Helm's Gate. Had it not been then for the arrival of the Rohirrim and Gandalf the White, Helm's Deep would surely have fallen and all its defenders and the refugees hiding in the Glittering Caves beneath its foundations would have been slaughtered.

Sauron's forces are bringing their own engines of war to this new battlefield, but they are

greater by far – both in size and effectiveness – than those which were manufactured in Saruman's factories of Isengard. From the vast pits beneath Barad-dûr, from its furnaces and foundries, and from the smithies of East Osgiliath, will come new horrors: siege towers of gigantic size hauled by armoured mountain-trolls and manned by hordes of Orcs, wherein the invaders can take safe cover as the towers are wheeled up to the walls of the city; massive catapults which can bear pitch and fire and stones.

And last of all, will come a mighty battering ram, greater by far than that which broke Helm's Gate; for the Gate of Gondor is strongly made indeed, wrought of steel and iron, and guarded with towers and bastions of stone: yet it is the weakest point in the city's defences. Grond is the name of this great engine of war, after the mace of the first Dark Lord, Morgoth, who once was Sauron's master; and it has been long in the making in Mordor. At over a hundred feet in length, it is as long as a forest tree and it swings on huge irons chains. Its

head is fashioned of black steel in the likeness of a ravening wolf, and fire shoots from its eyes. Four great beasts draw it, bull-headed and massive of body: terrors in themselves, for their like have never before been seen on Middle-earth. Mountain-trolls will wield it and Orcs will defend it; and the Witch-king of Angmar will direct its use.

HOBBITS AS HEROES

"The stars are veiled ... a storm is coming"

A great cloud hangs over all the land between Rohan and the Mountains of Shadow, and it is deepening. War has already begun. In such grim times, all must play their part, even folk as small as hobbits. Now it is the turn of Meriadoc Brandybuck and Peregrin Took – Merry and Pippin – to prove their true worth: for the first time in their lives, they must take separate paths and follow new masters, for Gandalf has removed Pippin to Minas Tirith for his own protection, after the young hobbit stole a look in the seeing-stone of Orthanc and thus attracted the attention of the Great Eye.

At only twenty-nine years of age – still four years short of his coming-of-age in Shire reckoning – Pippin is indeed very young; the youngest of the four companions who set out from Hobbiton. In Minas Tirith he is presented to Denethor, the Steward of Gondor, father to the man who fell trying to protect him and Merry from Saruman's Uruk-hai at Amon Hen. In a gesture of thanks for Boromir's

sacrifice, Pippin offers his service to Denethor, and is duly fitted out in the uniform of the Tower Guard, a great honour indeed.

Arrayed all in black and silver, he wears a hauberk of forged steel and a high silver helmet with small raven wings on either side, set with a silver star in the centre of the circlet. Above the mail he wears a short surcoat of black, and embroidered on the breast in silver is the White Tree of Gondor. It is the livery once worn by Faramir, Boromir's brother, when he was a child; and while his heart and will may be as strong as any grown man's, Pippin is still mistaken for a child as he walks the streets of Gondor's great city. But his first task in this uniform – though it is not a task entrusted by his new master – is to light the warning beacons at the summit of Mount Mindolluin and thus to summon aid; as in answer, the lights of the subsequent beacons can be seen over the White Mountains as far as Edoras.

"Here do I swear fealty and service to Gondor, in peace or war, in living or dying, from this hour henceforth, until my lord release me, or death take me."

Meanwhile, Merry finds himself amongst the Horse-lords of the Riddermark with King Théoden of Rohan, as the light of the warning beacon is seen and the King summons all able-bodied men to muster at Dunharrow for the long ride to Minas Tirith. Determined to play his part in the war, Merry bravely offers the service of his sword to Théoden, who receives the offer graciously, deeming that Merry shall henceforth be an Esquire of Rohan; and so he, like Pippin, is fitted out in the war-accoutrements of his new master: the finely-tooled leather armour of the Rohirrim, a helm and cloak.

"He knows not to what end he rides, yet if he knew he would still go on."

But at Dunharrow, great disappointment awaits him: the King releases him from his service and will take him no further, for it is from there three days' hard riding to the beleaguered city, and the horses of the Rohirrim are too large and too strong for one as small as a hobbit to manage on their own: he would only be a burden.

Resigned to his fate, Merry turns away; only to be swept up by an anonymous Rider and borne away to war.

41

THE SIEGE OF GONDOR

"Courage will now be your best defence against the storm that is at hand"

Outside the walls of Minas Tirith, Gondor's greatest city, Orcish armies mass, thousand upon thousand of them with their engines of war, each of them bearing flaming torches and an unquenchable hatred for their enemy. Above them swoop the Nazgûl, striking fear into their own troops as into the hearts of the defenders of Minas Tirith. The Army of Darkness hugely outnumbers the soldiery within; and with the reports of a great fleet of corsairs sailing north from the hostile city of Umbar, and the whereabouts of the Ringbearer unknown, the future looks grim indeed for the Free Peoples of Middle-earth.

42

But now Gandalf is conducting the defence of Minas Tirith; and he is indomitable. He commands that the defenders return to their stations, lined up along the battlements of the lower levels as they watch the Orc army, tens of thousands strong, come within range of the outer wall. The Orcish catapults throw down the gauntlet with an opening salvo, but instead of the usual shot or flaming ballast it is with a

new atrocity that they assault the Men of Gondor. With their siege towers, Sauron's army may make incursions into the lower levels of Minas Tirith; with burning pitch they may set fire to its ancient stonework; but terror is a far worse enemy than flame. In despair and fury, the Gondorians fire their great trebuchets out at the marauding Orcs, sending boulders raining down upon them, and archers loose their arrows from all seven levels of Minas Tirith's battlements.

Orcish archers return fire, and soon the air is black with the exchange of deadly missiles. Each side suffers under the devastating onslaught. Then siege towers are brought up to the walls of the city and a battering ram thuds into its gates, but to no avail. Until, that is, eight mountain-trolls and four great, bull-headed monsters draw in the massive wheeled battering ram, Grond.

Nothing could possibly withstand the onslaught of such an engine: even the steel- and iron-bound

gates of Minas Tirith are no match for the tempered steel and black sorcery of its evil wolf-head. It smashes the Gate of Gondor, and Orcs spill into the First Circle of the city, beneath the archway where no enemy has ever passed.

Gandalf leads a counterattack with Gondorian soldiers and there ensues fierce hand-to-hand fighting. All around, buildings are aflame. Fires rage unchecked in the First Circle: it is time to retreat to Second; and soon after that to the Third.

As the Lord of the Nazgûl, the Witch-king of Angmar, and his fell beast loom over Gandalf and Shadowfax in the Fourth Circle of the city, all hope seems to be lost.

But from the distance comes the faint ring of war-horns. Rohan has come!

THE BATTLE OF THE PELENNOR FIELDS

"Say to Denethor that in this hour the King of the Mark himself will come down to the land of Gondor, though may be he will not ride back."

Horns sound like a storm upon the plain and a thunder in the mountains: the Rohirrim have come to give aid to their old ally in this darkest of times. Théoden and Éomer ride together, uncle and nephew reunited at last, arrayed in the magnificent leather armour and the crested helmets of their people. The white horsetail plume on Éomer's helm floats in his speed; King Théoden gallops upon Snowmane, and his banner is a white horse upon a field of green. Their arrival is a glorious sight; a sight to set hope in the hearts of those who defend Minas Tirith, and to strike fear into the enemy.

46

From Dunharrow, the muster has brought six thousand spears; and though that is far less than King Théoden had hoped for, it is a war-like and fearsome army, for the Rohirrim are tough and grim and well-versed in the skills of war; and they have seen how with fire and sword the Shadow has already fallen upon their own people: they have scores to settle.

The Witch-king screeches and his mount rises into the air with a great flap of its wings as the six thousand Rohan horsemen step up onto the skyline.

Now ensues the greatest battle of the War of the Ring between the armies of Sauron – including Haradrim, Easterlings, Orcs and mûmakil – led by the Lord of the Nazgûl; and the forces of Minas Tirith, all those that could be mustered from the surrounding lands, joined by the forces of Osgiliath and Ithilien and the Riders of Rohan.

HEROIC DEEDS

"Ride now, ride now, ride to ruin and the world's ending!"

As the front of the first rank of the Rohirrim gallops into battle like a breaker crashing to the shore, the battle-fury of their forefathers runs through King Théoden and his men. War-horns blast out; sunlight gleams off helm and weaponry. Nothing can withstand that first charge. An entire company of Orcs vanishes beneath trampling hooves. But having overcome the first wave of Orcs, there are ever more; and then Haradrim, and mûmakil, bearing huge war-towers packed with Haradrim archers, which bellow as they are driven mercilessly to war by their Harad masters. They lumber into the sea of men, trampling and crushing riders and horses beneath their vast feet, impaling the hapless upon their spiked tusks, as rains of Harad arrows fall all around.

48

Then it is that the Lord of the Nazgûl, the Witch-king of Angmar, swoops down and his fell beast grabs up in its cruel claws both Théoden and his white stallion, Snowmane; and thus comes the death of the valiant King of Rohan.

in disguise, driven by her desire for battle and her love for the Lord Aragorn. Now she – and the hobbit whom she has borne all the way from the Muster – will try to avenge King Théoden's death, or they will die in the attempt.

"Do not come between the Nazgûl and his prey!"

Then an unnamed Rider steps into the breach and with a single sweep of his shining sword beheads the vile monster on which the Witch-king is mounted. It is an act of extraordinary courage: for surely none can withstand the Lord of the Nazgûl; indeed, ancient prophecy has foretold such, deeming that no living man can kill him. Yet the Witch-king of Angmar's antagonist is no mere man, but Éowyn: valorous shieldmaiden of Rohan and niece of the fallen king, who has ridden from Dunharrow

THE BLACK GATE

Once the Battle of the Pelennor Fields is won – more by the dead than the living – all that is left for Aragorn and his allies to aid the quest to destroy the Ring is to confront the Dark Lord in his own realm, and thus draw his attention away from Sam and Frodo as they make their lonely, desperate way into the Land of Shadow.

After the slaughter on the Pelennor Fields, their numbers are perilously few: they stand no chance of victory against the mighty army which Sauron still maintains within the Black Gate, the great iron rampart across the haunted pass into Mordor at the meeting of the Ephel Dúath (The Mountains of Shadow) and the Ered Lithui (the Ashen Mountains).

"What did they bring, the Kings of old?

From over the sundered seas?

Seven stars, and seven stones

And one white tree…"

Wearing the armour of his forebears, with the White Tree of Gondor on his chest, and bearing the Sword Reforged, Aragorn, once known as Strider, leads the remainder of the Nine Companions and the Captains of the West to what must surely be their deaths…

THE LIEUTENANT OF THE TOWER

"His name is remembered in no tale…"

At the Gate they cry out a challenge; a challenge which will be answered by one of the Dark

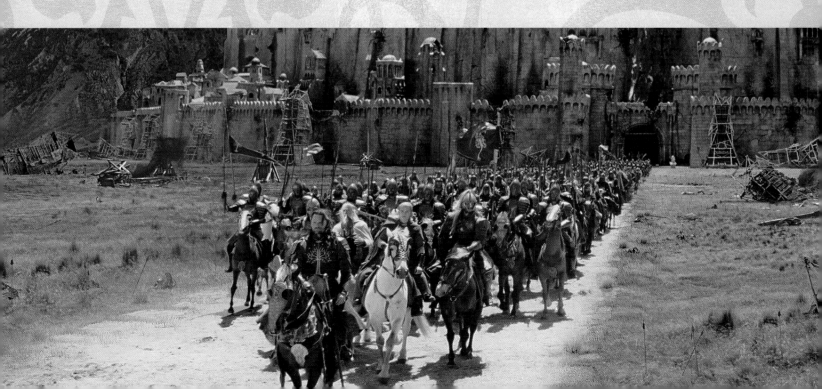

Lord's chief servants. The apparition who rides out to meet them is the Lieutenant of the Dark Tower of Barad-dûr, a creature of sorcery now grown advanced in evil and cruel cunning. For so long has he served his master that he no longer bears his own name, but is known merely as the Mouth of Sauron. He rides a huge and hideous black horse with a face like a frightful mask, more like a skull than a living head, and eyes of flame; and his own visage is hardly more fair.

Gleeful and arrogant, the Mouth of Sauron delivers to the brave visitors the false tidings that the Ringbearer has been apprehended by the Orcs of Cirith Ungol and taken to the torture chambers of the Dark Tower. In evidence of this, he flourishes the mithril shirt taken from Frodo, and a great despair engulfs them.

Moments later, drums beat out and fires flare up. The Black Gate of Mordor swings open, and a vast army of Orcs marches out.

"There may come a day when the courage of Men fails… an hour of wolves before the Age of Men comes crashing down – but it will not be this day! This day we fight!"

51

THE TREACHERY OF GOLLUM

"We hates them, nassty hobbitses..."

As Sam and Frodo make their slow, painful, perilous journey across the forsaken places of Middle-earth on their quest to destroy the One Ring in the fires of Mount Doom – the one place in the world where it can be unmade – they are accompanied by one who claims to be able to aid their safe passage into Mordor.

Gollum – who used to be called Sméagol, a creature much like a hobbit – has a long and strange history: for he too was a Ringbearer, of sorts, for many, many years. Having murdered his cousin Déagol to acquire the golden trinket they found while out fishing, Sméagol fell under the malevolent influence of the Ring and wandered away from his homeland to take refuge from the light in the caves beneath the Misty Mountains. And it was there where he finally lost his 'Precious' to Frodo's uncle, Bilbo Baggins.

"Master carries heavy burden ... Smeagol knows: Smeagol carried burden many years"

Now, the two parts of him – Sméagol, who still vaguely remembers the time when he was not the slave of the Ring and is able to experience feelings which have not been entirely warped and wicked; and Gollum, whose only wish is to take back the Ring for himself and see the thieves who carry it now dead and rotting – are warring for dominance of his soul. Shall he lead the hobbits, as he has promised, via safe ways into the Land of Shadow; or shall he lead them to destruction and then reunite himself with the Precious?

"Treachery, treachery I fear; Treachery of that miserable creature!"

Frodo's apparent treachery in allowing Faramir and his rangers to take Gollum prisoner in Ithilien has weighted the scales: now the personality of Sméagol has been subsumed by the ravening greed of Gollum. He cannot kill the two hobbits himself: no, for the Fat One is strong and bears a dreaded Elven rope which chokes and burns.

But if he cannot do the deed himself, he knows one who can. So it is through Morgul Vale and up the Stair of Cirith Ungol that Gollum leads the hobbits. It is not a way they would have chosen, had they known what lay ahead...

MINAS MORGUL

"That accursed valley passed into evil
a very long time ago"

Minas Ithil – the Tower of the Moon – was once the fortress-city of Isildur, son of Elendil. It was built high in an upland valley beneath the Mountains of Shadow, on the road which runs south out of the fair lands of Ithilien, and in its day it was a city both beautiful and bright, and the Moon lit its inner courts with a wondrous silver light.

But in the early part of the Third Age, the Tower of the Moon was lost to Sauron's forces and became the lair of the Nazgûl, the Nine Ringwraiths; and then it became known as Minas Morgul, the Tower of Black Sorcery. Now it has the radiance of corpse-light: a faint, ailing, noisome green, and in its walls and towers windows show like countless holes all looking inward, to emptiness and ruin.

"Ruined city, yes, very nasty place,
full of enemies"

A road leads out of the dead city, crossing a bridge adorned with the carved forms of people and beasts, all of them loathsome and corrupt. Beneath the bridge, the water steams with vile and poisonous fumes; and all about the meads on either side of the stream luminous white flowers glow with an eerie, charnel beauty. It is a grim and unnerving place, even without the shrieking presence of the Nazgûl; or the vast army of Orcs which issues from its cavernous doors...

THE PASS OF CIRITH UNGOL

near-vertical stairway has been cut into the sheer rock which leads upward from the gate of Minas Morgul into the dizzying heights above and up to the only pass which leads through the Mountains of Shadow. The pass is guarded by the Tower of Cirith Ungol, and the way is perilous; not only because the stairs are treacherous and the tower manned by vicious Orcs – but for the unseen horror which gives both pass and tower their name, did the hobbits but know it.

Up the stairs Gollum leads Frodo and Sam. The steps are worn and smooth, narrow and unevenly spaced. Some are already broken, or crack if a foot is set upon them. They are so great and so steep that the hobbits – smaller creatures than this stairway was first made for – climb them as if climbing an endless ladder, a ladder which stretches for two thousand feet from the valley floor into the mists above.

It is hard not to look down, hard to ignore the chill void at their heels which beckons every misstep; but still Gollum clambers upward, and all they can do is follow.

58

At the top of the ridge lies the Tower of Cirith Ungol: a great three-tiered watch-tower and fortress now garrisoned by Orcs from both Barad-dûr and Minas Morgul. As the hobbits climb, they can see the Tower silhouetted in the cleft between the mountains, guarding the way both in and out of Mordor; beyond it, far out on the Plain of Gorgoroth, lies Barad-dûr, with its iron crown and Lidless Eye. The dull, red light which can be spied through the cleft comes from Orodruin – the Mountain of Fire; Mount Doom itself – as great gouts of volcanic flame erupt from its peak.

But the way is guarded not only by Orcs, but also by the Two Watchers: two sentient statues of stone emanating great evil. Each of the statues boasts three vulture-heads, and each head faces inward, outward and across the gateway, ready to sound an alarm if any intruder or spy should pass.

SHELOB

"Let her deal with them ... she must eat. All she gets is filthy orcses.
She hungers for sweeter meats'

At the top of the stair at Cirith Ungol there lies a ravine through tall grey weathered rock. Gollum insists that the tunnels which lie within this ravine represent the only safe way through to the other side of the mountains: for the Pass is too vigilantly guarded – by the Two Watchers and the Orc garrison – for them to take that route. The mouth of this cavern emits a foul stench. Inside is utmost darkness.

Through an upward-leading tunnel they go, passing tributary passages which they sense rather than see in this lightless place. There is nothing in here but an ominous silence, yet Frodo senses some lurking malice; and, oddly, the walls are sticky to the touch.

"There's something worse than Gollum about. I can feel something looking at us."

Gollum's treachery is revealed. For the cavern into which he has led them is the lair of a vile and ancient horror...

"Long had she been hungry, lurking in her den"

Shelob, the occupant of this rank catacomb, has dwelt here for millennia, before even Sauron came to Middle-earth, weaving webs of shadow in which to trap her prey and gorging herself on unwitting travellers – on Elves and Men who happened in her way; then on beasts which knew no better than to avoid her lair. In all this agelong time she has grown vast and bloated and bitter; but since the city below the Pass fell into ruin and became the haunt of the Nazgûl, her prey has also waned: now all she feeds upon is the odd unwary Orc.

Gollum happened upon this horror during his escape from Sauron's torture chambers, hundreds of years ago; ever since, she has lurked in his mind. Now, his plan to regain the One Ring may be fulfilled, for Shelob has no appetite for gold or power; only for flesh. Once she has trapped Frodo and eaten his poor body, the Ring will fall unregarded to the ground. And then Gollum may be reunited with his Precious...

As they penetrate deeper into the dark tunnels, there comes a venomous hissing sound; and Gollum flees, deserting the hobbits, he had promised to guide safely through the mountains to Mordor. A pale green light begins to illuminate the tunnel. Now the true depth of

THE COURAGE OF SAMWISE GAMGEE

"No onslaught more fierce was ever seen in the savage world of beasts…"

Samwise Gamgee is a gardener, and the son of a gardener. Before this long and arduous journey, he had never even left the Shire, let alone wielded a sword or faced an enemy. But his love and loyalty for his master, Frodo Baggins, has brought him a very long way from the lush pastures and comfortable inns of his home.

Sam would never have considered himself brave, or any sort of hero. He was always quite content with his lot; could not even raise the nerve to ask lovely Rosie Cotton for a dance. But now he has stayed with the Elves in Rivendell and Lothlórien, travelled through the legendary Mines of Moria, traversed meres and mountains, seen Oliphaunts and ruined cities, fought Black Riders and Cave Trolls, Orcs and Uruk-hai.

But in all those matters he had little or no choice: his duty was to Frodo, and he followed blindly. Even facing the most appalling monster he has encountered so far – with her many knobbed and steely legs, her vile clusters of eyes and wicked mandibles; her vast, bloated

body and venomous claws – is not his greatest test; for the rage that surges up inside him when he sees what she has done to his beloved Frodo overtakes all reason. No: the most severe test of his extraordinary courage has yet to come.

"I have something to do before the end. I must see it through…"

When he thinks his master dead and that all is lost, nothing would be so easy as to give up, to succumb to despair: to flee that awful place and somehow make his way back to the Shire, alone and grieving. But the Great Task still remains; and if Sam will not carry it through, there is no one left alive who can.

It is a brave decision, to take the Ring; and in doing so, Sam saves the entire quest. If he had not, the Orcs would have scavenged it from Frodo's body and taken it to Sauron, and shadow would have fallen over all the world. He may berate himself for believing his master dead – amidst all the horror and the carnage – when he is merely poisoned and paralysed; but this error, and his courage, have turned back a tide of evil.

AMONG THE ORCS

In the midst of hostile territory, surrounded by thousands of Orcs and with the Lidless Eye searching constantly for the hobbit who bears the One Ring, Frodo and Sam are faced by a dilemma as they make their escape from the Tower of Cirith Ungol and their entry into the Land of Shadow, for Frodo's garments and belongings have been appropriated and squabbled over by the Tower Guards, and Sam has only his cloak to spare. But some of the Orcs who garrisoned the Tower are very little taller than the two hobbits, and so, although they may be disgusted by the rank stench of the enemy soldiers and appalled at having to scavenge raiment from the dead, Orc-armour and breeches it must be if they are to enter Mordor. Besides, the bizarre helmets will shield the faces of folk who look very little like the denizens of that grim place. It is a very effective disguise: too effective, maybe.

As the hobbits struggle across the foothills, they find themselves face to face with a large battalion of Orcs and are whipped into line by the overseer of that troop, and after a painful forced march soon find themselves in the midst of a vast Orc-army – hundreds of thousands of enemy soldiers encamped on the Gorgoroth Plain, ready to annihilate the remnants of the armies of Gondor and Rohan under Aragorn's command. Drums beat and torches flare in the night. Unspeakable things roast over campfires. All of Middle-earth will soon look like this – blighted and abused – unless Frodo's quest succeeds.

Orodruin, the Mountain of Fire – the final destination for the destruction of the One Ring – is clearly visible now through the brooding, ashladen skies…

65

MOUNT DOOM

"There is no veil between me and the wheel of fire. I see it even with my waking eyes…'

Far across the Gorgoroth Plain, that giant volcano – Orodruin, the Mountain of Fire – is erupting. It casts great streams of ash and lava high into the air, illuminating the thick cloud which hangs over Mordor with a flickering, fiery orange light.

The closer Sam and Frodo approach, dragging their desperate, weary feet ever onward, the more violent and hellish their surroundings become: red heat hisses out of fissures, everywhere the rocks are jagged and razor-sharp, choking volcanic ash blankets the land; terrifying red lightning forks across the sky.

For these Shire folk, used to the soft greens and blues of a gentle, rainwashed rural landscape,

with its rolling pastures and flower-filled meadows, its millponds and woodlands, it must look like the very end of the world.

With the Ring burdening him ever more cruelly, by the time they reach the foot of the mountain, Frodo will be reduced to crawling on his hands and knees. Thousands of feet above them the volcano towers, its summit wreathed in fiery cloud. Even for two strong, able-bodied Men, the climb would be a feat. For two exhausted and traumatized hobbits at the very end of their resources – both physical and mental – it represents what appears an impossible task. Far, far above is the stone doorway of the Sammath Naur, which leads into the Crack of Doom – that great, lava-filled chasm in which Sauron first forged the One Ring, and the only place in all the world where it, and all its evil, can be unmade. Yet all this remains shrouded to them; as does the third creature which toils up this grim and vertiginous slope…

"Wicked Baggins!
Mustn't go that way,
mustn't hurt Precious!'

FRODO'S CHOICE

"Destroy it now ... throw it into the fire!"

Never has any mortal in possession of a Ring of Power relinquished it willingly. Even the lesser Rings have claimed the essence of their wearers, reducing them to monstrous wraiths, incorporeal in the world they wished to rule, their souls bound to the service of the Dark Lord, who seduced them with lies and then enslaved them.

But the One Ring – the Ring which rules all other Rings of Power – has an evil force all its own, and contains a large part of Sauron's dark magic. Isildur, son of Elendil, King of Gondor, struck the One Ring from Sauron's hand and cast him down in the battle which ended the Second Age of Middle-earth; but when he climbed Mount Doom to destroy the artefact as urged by Lord Elrond of the Elves, his will failed him, and he kept the Ring, to his own undoing; a failure which led to the fall of his line and, hundreds of years later, to the War of the Ring.

Bilbo Baggins found it most difficult and painful to lose the Ring; and aged as soon as it left him. Gandalf felt its presence and – for all his might and lore – dared not touch the One Ring for fear of the corruption it might work upon him. Galadriel, the Lady of the Golden Wood, who already held Nenya, one of the three Rings forged for the Elves, had the chance to take the Ruling Ring from Frodo in Lothlórien, but would not accept it for knowledge that it would render her most terrible. Boromir fell beneath its spell, and would have taken it as his own; his brother Faramir proved stronger; but their father, Denethor craved the power it represents.

But of all things, it is the creature once called Sméagol who best knows the seductive power of the One Ring. Warped by the proximity of his 'Precious', 'Sméagol' has been subsumed by 'Gollum', who has forgotten all that was ever good or gentle in his being: the loss of the Ring has caused him such intense pain and avarice that he is determined to regain it, no matter what the price.

Frodo must enter the chambers of the Sammath Naur and cast the One Ring into the boiling lava of the Crack of Doom, the fissure which lies far below. In doing so, he must relinquish the vast potential of the Ruling Ring, all its seductive power and might. It will require immense strength of will to carry his great quest through to the end.

"I have made my choice…"

68

HarperCollins*Publishers*
77–85 Fulham Palace Road,
Hammersmith, London W6 8JB
www.tolkien.co.uk

Published by HarperCollins*Publishers* 2003
1 3 5 7 9 8 6 4 2

Photographs: Pierre Vinet & Chris Coad
Editor: Chris Smith
Design: Terence Caven
Production: Arjen Jansen

A catalogue record for this book
is available from the British Library

ISBN 0 00 711626 8

Set in Slimbach

Printed and bound by Proost NV, Turnhout,
Belgium